I0801176

I READ! YOU READ!

Child's Turn to Read

Adult's Turn to Read

WE READ ABOUT

SPORTS CARS

By Ryan James and Azi Chandra

SEAHORSE PUBLISHING

Parent and Caregiver Guide

Reading aloud with your child has many benefits. It expands vocabulary, sparks discussion, and promotes an emotional bond. Research shows that children who have books read aloud to them have improved language skills, leading to greater school success.

I Read! You Read! books offer a fun and easy way to read with your child. Follow these guidelines.

Before Reading

- Look at the front and back covers. Discuss personal experiences that relate to the topic. Make predictions about the book.
- Scan the *Glossary* at the back of the book. Talk about any words that are new to your child
- If the book will be challenging or unfamiliar to your child, read it aloud by yourself the first time. Then, invite your child to participate in a second reading.

During Reading

CHILD Have your child read the words beside this symbol. This text has been carefully matched to the reading and grade levels shown on the cover.

ADULT You read the words beside this symbol.

- Stop often to discuss what you are reading and to make sure your child understands.
- If your child struggles with decoding a word, help them sound it out. If it is still a challenge, say the word for your child and have them repeat it after you.
- To find the meaning of a word, look for clues in the surrounding words and pictures.

After Reading

- Praise your child's efforts. Notice how they have grown as a reader.
- Use the *After Reading Questions* at the back of the book.
- Discuss what your child learned and what they liked or didn't like about the book.

Most importantly, let your child know that reading is fun and worthwhile. Keep reading together as your child's skills and confidence grow.

TABLE OF CONTENTS

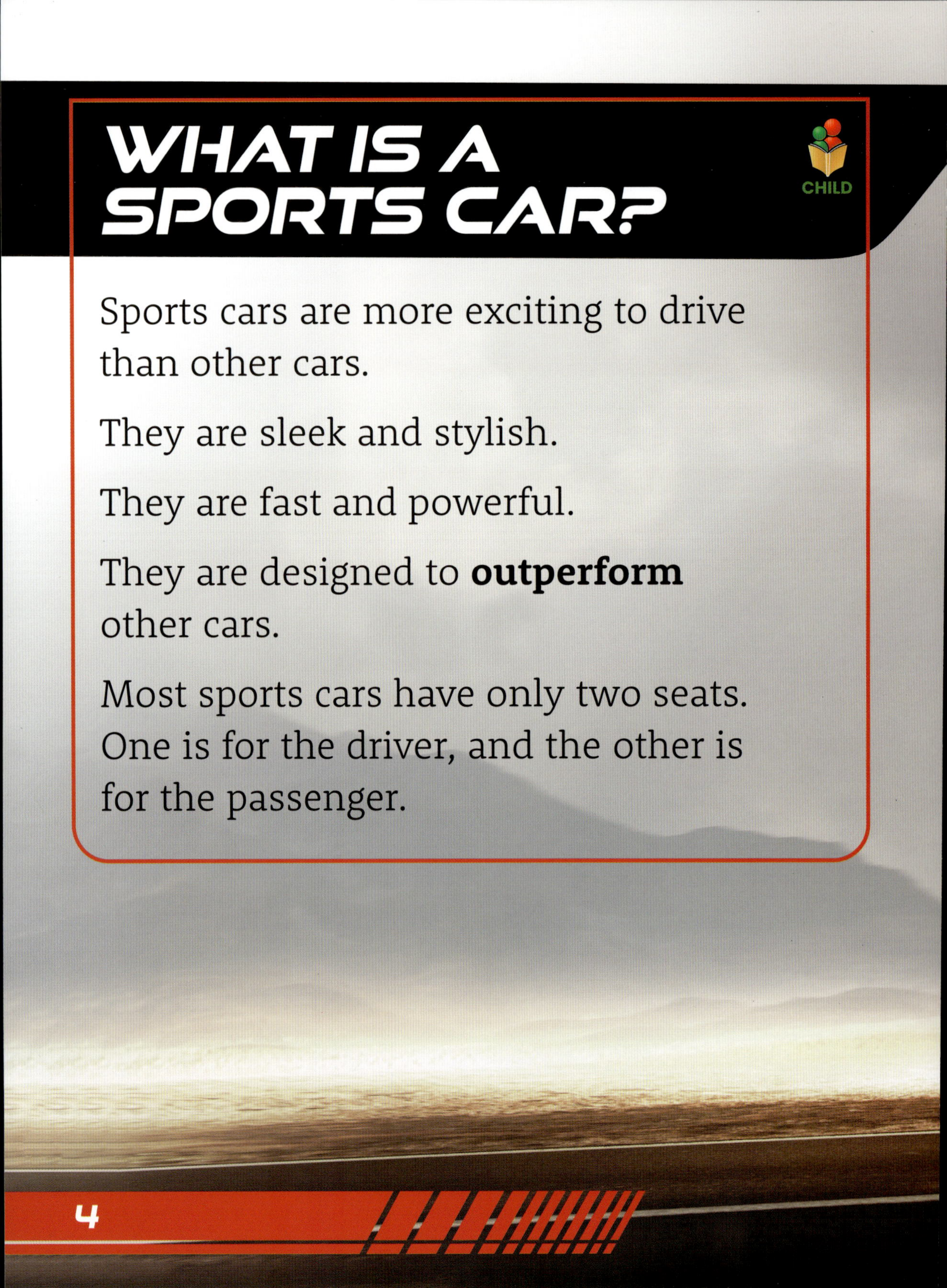

WHAT IS A SPORTS CAR?

Sports cars are more exciting to drive than other cars.

They are sleek and stylish.

They are fast and powerful.

They are designed to **outperform** other cars.

Most sports cars have only two seats. One is for the driver, and the other is for the passenger.

THE FIRST SPORTS CARS

ADULT

In the 1920s, British **manufacturers** such as the Triumph Motor Company created the first sports cars.

Some car races at this time had cars go up unpaved hills.

Sports cars were the best at these types of races.

FUN FACTS

The Ferrari logo came from an Italian World War I fighter pilot named Count Francesco Baracca who painted a similar logo on his plane.

SPORTS CARS BECOME POPULAR

ADULT

During World War II, American soldiers were sent to fight in Europe.

When they arrived, they saw sports cars and started driving them.

They liked how they looked and how simple they were to drive.

After the war, European companies such as Porsche started selling sports cars in the United States.

SPORTS CAR PARTS

ADULT

Some sports cars have 12-cylinder **internal combustion engines**.

Other sports cars have electric or hybrid engines.

Many sports car engines get extra power from the addition of a **turbocharger**.

Wheels on sports cars are bigger than on other cars. Performance tires are designed to get better **traction** on the road.

FUN FACTS

The record-setting Koenigsegg Gemera can go from 0 to 60 miles (0 to 96.5 kilometers) per hour in only 1.9 seconds.

AMERICAN SPORTS CARS

ADULT

Some sports cars are made in the United States.

Popular models are the Chevrolet Corvette, the Ford Mustang, and the Dodge Charger.

Powerful American-made sports cars can reach speeds of nearly 200 miles (322 kilometers) per hour.

But they may not be as **luxurious** as European sports cars.

EUROPEAN SPORTS CARS

ADULT

Some sports cars are made in European countries such as Italy and Germany.

Models include the Lamborghini Aventador, the Audi R8, and the Ferrari 458 Italia.

Some of these cars go super-fast, but they are not allowed to be driven on regular roads.

They can cost one million dollars or more.

FUN FACTS

The 1962 Ferrari 250 GTO was the most expensive car sold at an auction. It sold for 48.4 million dollars in 2018.

SPORTS CARS IN ACTION

NASCAR (National Association for Stock Car Auto Racing) uses sports cars in their races.

The most common sports cars used in these races are the Ford Mustang and the Chevrolet Camaro.

These cars are built to be **aerodynamic** and to have good traction on sharp turns.

CAR SHOWS

Manufacturers show their new sports cars at car shows.

Car **enthusiasts** can look at a variety of vehicles all in one place. People can sit inside the cars or even drive them.

Drivers get to see the newest, fastest, most exciting sports cars.

EXIT
EXIT

TOP MODELS

AMERICAN

Chevrolet Corvette

First year in production: 1953

Average price: $67,000

Top speed: 194 mph (312 kph)

Chevrolet Camaro

First year in production: 1966

Average price: $30,000

Top speed: 202 mph (325 kph)

Ford Mustang

First year in production: 1964

Average price: $30,000

Top speed: 186 mph (299 kph)

EUROPEAN

Lamborghini Aventador

First year in production: 2011
Average price: $400,000
Top speed: 220 mph (355 kph)

Bugatti Chiron

First year in production: 2016
Average price: $3,000,000
Top speed: 305 mph (491 kph)

Ferrari 458 Italia

First year in production: 2009
Average price: $250,000
Top speed: 210 mph (340 kph)

GLOSSARY

aerodynamic (air-oh-dye-NAM-ik): having a shape that moves through air quickly and easily

enthusiasts (en-THOO-zee-ists): people who are passionate about a particular subject or activity

internal combustion engines (in-TUR-nuhl kuhm-BUS-chuhn EN-jins): machines that make cars move by burning gasoline in an enclosed space, producing hot gases that drive pistons

luxurious (lugh-ZHOOR-ee-uhs): comfortable, elegant, and expensive

manufacturers (man-yuh-FAK-chur-uhrs): companies that make products in a factory

outperform (out-pur-FORM): to work better than what is standard or ordinary

traction (TRAK-shuhn): the force that keeps a moving body from slipping on a surface, such as a moving tire on a road

turbocharger (TUR-boh-chahrj-uhr): a blower driven by exhaust gas turbines that is used to increase the power of an engine

INDEX

AFTER READING QUESTIONS

1. When did sports cars become popular in the United States?
2. How are sports cars different from other cars?
3. Why might a sports car be very expensive?
4. Why are sports cars used in NASCAR racing?
5. Where can drivers learn about new sports cars?

Written by: Ryan James and Azi Chandra
Design by: Kathy Walsh
Editor: Kim Thompson

Photographs/Shutterstock: Cover & Title Pg ©Chevrolet, ©Urse Major, ©Mooam, ©VoodooDot; Pg 3, 6, 8, 10, 12, 14, 16, 20, 22 ©Urse Major; Pg 7, 11, 15 ©Mooam; Pg 4 ©CParabolStudio; Pg 5 ©imtmphoto; Pg 6 ©FernandoV; Pg 7 ©Frank11; Pg 8 ©Massimo Campanari; Pg 9 ©Everyonephoto Studio; Pg 10 ©EA Photography; Pg 11 ©Erik Cox Photography; Pg 12 ©Ken Morris; Pg 13 ©Kevin Tichenor; Pg 14 ©Tom B Paye; Pg 15 ©Dan74; Pg 16 ©Grindstone Media Group; Pg 17 ©Art Konovalov; Pg 19 ©Chatchai Somwat; Pg 20 ©Clari Massimiliano, ©Steve Lagreca, ©Sarunyu L; Pg 21 ©PhatTai, ©supermodel, ©Roman.S-Photographer

Library of Congress PCN Data
We Read About Sports Cars / Ryan James and Azi Chandra
I Read! You Read!
ISBN 979-8-8873-5918-2 (hard cover)
ISBN 979-8-8873-5957-1 (paperback)
ISBN 979-8-8904-2016-9 (EPUB)
ISBN 979-8-8904-2075-6 (eBook)
Library of Congress Control Number: 2023912461

Printed in China.

Seahorse Publishing Company
www.seahorsepub.com

Copyright © 2024 **SEAHORSE PUBLISHING COMPANY**

All rights reserved. No part of this publication may be reproduced, stored in a retrieval system or be transmitted in any form or by any means, electronic, mechanical, photocopying, recording, or otherwise, without the prior written permission of Seahorse Publishing Company.

Published in the United States
Seahorse Publishing
PO Box 771325
Coral Springs, FL 33077

SEAHORSE PUBLISHING